To Ra,
Enjoy your reading,
Remember to question
everything!
Fayola

This book details slave rebellions carried out by brave people who believed in freedom. Although the majority of revolts were unsuccessful the courageous acts of slaves encouraged abolition movements that eventually led to the end of slavery. This book reflects on some of the most infamous rebellions. There are many more which should also be celebrated.

1
Maroon rebellion

Dates: 1728 – 1740
Location: Jamaica/Guyana

Details: After being enslaved by European colonists, many slaves escaped to mountains. Free communities developed in the mountains and those that tried to recapture them were attacked.

Importance: The Maroon's went on to invade plantations and free slaves. They maintained their legacy and lived independently from plantations.

Keywords: The Leeward and Windward Peace treaties of 1739 were developed to end this revolt. Peace Treaties are agreements created to end a war.

Maroon is a Spanish term given to free slaves which meant unruly.

2

Berbice Slave Uprising

Dates: 23rd February 1763
Location: Berbice, Guyana

Details: Led by the slave, Cuffy the rebellion sought possession of half of Berbice. This uprising lasted for over a year and came to an end due to internal disputes amongst the rebels as well as external factors.

Importance: The uprising was almost successful in setting up a Maroon community. Both African born and Creole slaves worked together for a period during this uprising.

Keywords: Creole person is of mixed European and African descent. Can also relate to language of slaves in the Caribbean which is a mix of European and African languages.

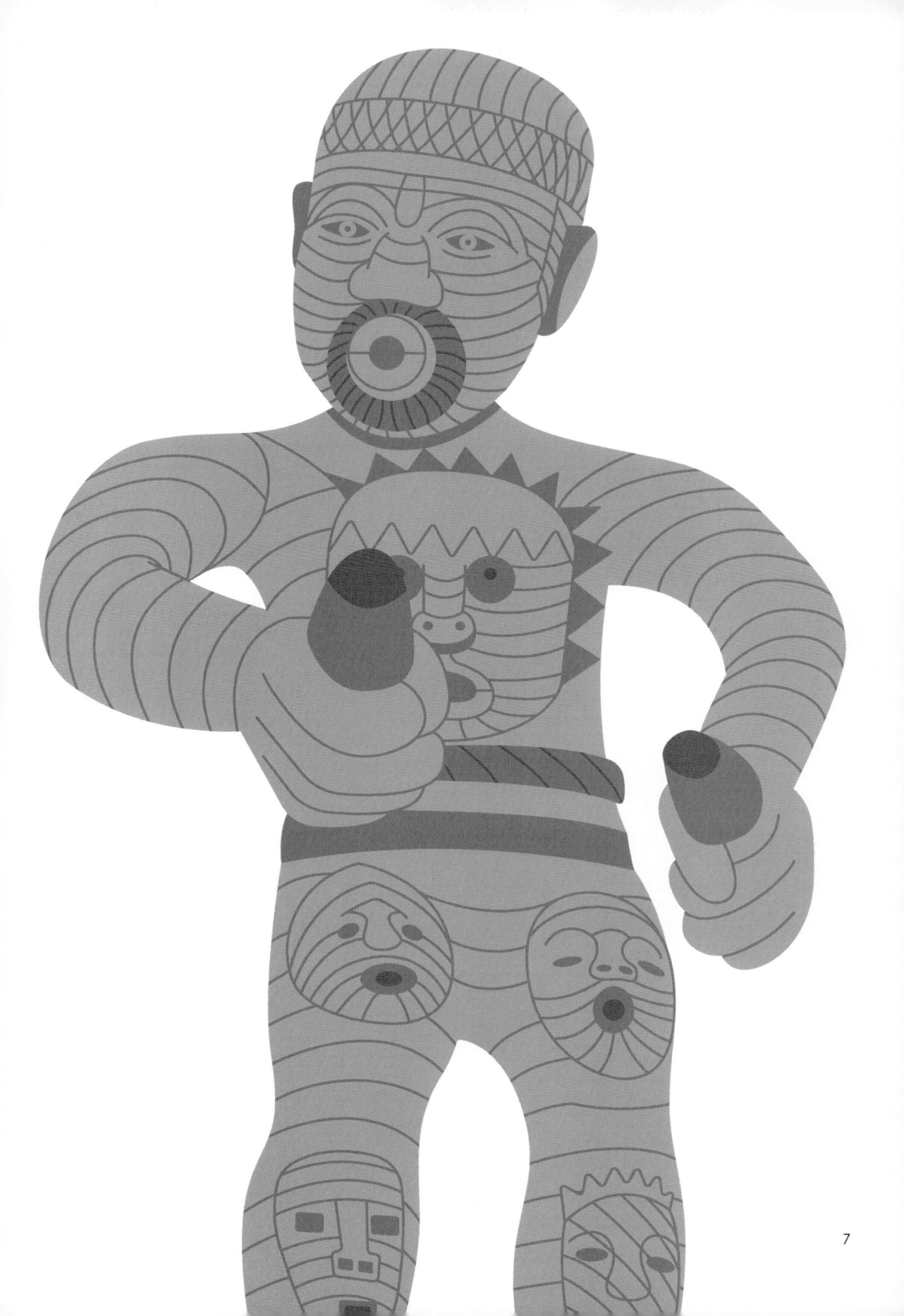

3

Toussaint Louverture

Dates: 1791 – 1794
Location: Haiti

Details: Known for his role in the Haitian Revolution, Toussaint began this uprising in Saint Dominque when he was a free black man. The success of his rebellion managed to gain paid work for slaves on plantations. The Haitian Revolution began as a result of the rebellion which saw Haiti defeating countries such as France and the United Kingdom.

Importance: The Saint Dominque uprising helped to inspire other rebellions.
(See page 10).

Keywords: Black Jacobin – The Jacobin era relates to the 1600s. Black Jacobin's were black men and women who were of great importance and high social status at the time.

4

German Coast Uprising

Dates: January 8 – 10th 1811
Location: Louisiana

Details: Charles Deslondes led this revolt. It is believed that this revolt was inspired by the Haitian Revolution (see page 8).

Importance: The German Coast Uprising is the largest slave revolt in American history. Almost 500 slaves were involved.

Keywords: The rebellion is named the German Coast Uprising due to the heavily German populated area in Louisiana, where it took place.

Drapetomania was thought to be a mental illness suffered by slaves, causing them to run away.

5

Bussa (slave) Bussa Rebellion

Dates: 14th – 16th April 1816
Location: Barbados

Details: Bussa was a head officer at the Bayley plantation. Slaves on this plantation were captured by Europeans. The slaves believed that this rebellion would help with the abolition movement.

Importance: This rebellion has been recognised for its importance in the abolition of slavery. The Bussa Emancipation Statue was erected in Barbados in 1985.

6

Demerara Rebellion

Dates: August 1823
Location: Guyana/South America

Details: Slaves on the Plantation Success began to discuss a rebellion. The leaders were a father and son duo, Jack Gladstone (son) and Quamina Gladstone (father).

Importance: Over 10,000 slaves were involved in the rebellion. Quamina was a deacon at an English missionary church. The slaves involved in this rebellion were educated and literate.

Keywords: Deacon – a minister in a church. English missionaries – person/people sent by a church to help/educate people who are often disadvantaged. They often share religious ideas with people.

7

Nat Turner

Dates: 21st August 1831
Location: Virginia

Details: Nat Turner claimed to have been encouraged to lead this rebellion as a spirit had spoken to him and told him to do so. He was educated and led Bible sermons. His followers on the plantation took part in the rebellion also.

Importance: It is believed that this rebellion led to the Civil Rights Movement. His testimony, upon being caught, is compelling and has given a voice to slaves who largely were voiceless.

8

Sam Sharpe Revolt

Dates: 25th December 1831
Location: Jamaica

Details: Samuel Sharpe was named after the plantation owner which was on the parish of St James. Slaves decided to stop working on Christmas Day. This marked the beginning of the Sam Sharpe Revolt.

Importance: Sam Sharpe was a travelling black Baptist deacon. He is known as a national hero of Jamaica and can be seen on the $50 note.

9

Amistad

Dates: August 1839
Location: New York

Details: This extraordinary revolt took place on board a Spanish slave ship. The illegally captured slaves took over the ship by defeating the captain and crew. John Cinque and Serge Pieh unchained themselves and led the revolt.

Importance: The revolt caught the attention of abolitionists which led to a court case. Slaves were freed and they returned back to their homeland of Sierra Leone. The revolt has come alive on screen with a film released by the name of Amistad.

10
Akwamu Slave Revolt

Dates: 23rd November 1733
Location: St John

Details: Akwamu slaves were originally from Ghana and were taken to the Caribbean, specifically St John. They revolted against their Danish captures due to inhumane treatment and conditions. The aim was to take control of the plantation.

Importance: An African female, Breffu, was one of the leaders of the revolt. The revolt was one of the longest lasting slave revolts on record. It lasted for 6 months ending in 1734.

Bonus hero
Harriet Tubman

Dates: 1822 – 1913

Details: Harriet Tubman first freed herself from slavery by running away from her master. She then went on to free thousands of slaves, helping them to escape through 'The Underground Railroad' where slaves were kept safe until they reached the North of America.

Importance: Harriet Tubman was an abolitionist and a nurse during the Civil War. She has been called 'Moses' and 'General Tubman' for her courageous efforts in the abolition of slavery.

References/Bibliography

1 – Martin, S.I. (2000) Britain's Slave Trade 2nd Edition, London Channel 4 Books Wikipedia.org. Available at: https://en.wikipedia.org/wiki/First_Maroon_War https://cyber.harvard.edu/eon/marroon/history.html

2 – Knight, Franklin W (1997) General History of the Caribbean, Volume III: The slave societies of the Caribbean, London, Unesco/Macmillan publishing

3 – Forsdick C & Hogsbjerg C (2017) Toussaint Louverture: A Black Jacobean in the age of Revolutions, London, Pluto Press

4 – Momodu, S (2007) Blackpast.org. Available at: https://www.blackpast.org/african-american-history/andry-s-rebellion-1811/

5 – Thenationalarchives.gov.uk. Available at: https://www.nationalarchives.gov.uk/education/resources/bussas-rebellion/

6 – Momodu, S (2017) Blackpast.org. Available at: https://www.blackpast.org/global-african-history/demerara-rebellion-1823/

7 – Baker K (2008, 2016) Nat Turner, United States of America, Abrams ComicArts

8 - Martin, S.I. (2000) Britain's Slave Trade 2nd Edition, London, Channel 4 Books

9 – History.com Editors (2010) History.com. Available at: https://www.history.com/this-day-in-history/supreme-court-rules-on-amistad-mutiny

10 – Black Star News (2021) Blackstarnews.com. Available at: https://www.blackstarnews.com/education/education/the-akwamu-slave-revolt-of-1733-on-st-john.html

Bonus hero – Wallenfeldt, J (2021) Britannica.com. Available at: https://www.britannica.com/biography/Harriet-Tubman

Printed in Great Britain
by Amazon